52 THINGS TO DO WHILE YOU POO

THE FART EDITION

AN HACHETTE UK COMPANY
WWW.HACHETTE.CO.UK

SUMMERSDALE PUBLISHERS LTD
PART OF OCTOPUS PUBLISHING GROUP LIMITED
CARMELITE HOUSE
50 VICTORIA EMBANKMENT
LONDON
EC4Y 0DZ
UK

WWW.SUMMERSDALE.COM
PRINTED AND BOUND IN CHINA
ISBN: 978-1-78685-996-9

SUBSTANTIAL DISCOUNTS ON BULK QUANTITIES OF SUMMERSDALE BOOKS
ARE AVAILABLE TO CORPORATIONS, PROFESSIONAL ASSOCIATIONS AND
OTHER ORGANIZATIONS. FOR DETAILS CONTACT GENERAL ENQUIRIES:
TELEPHONE: +44 (0) 1243 771107 OR EMAIL: ENQUIRIES@SUMMERSDALE.COM.

52 THINGS TO DO WHILE YOU POO

THE FART EDITION

HUGH JASSBURN

52 THINGS TO DO WHILE YOU POO

ROARING FROM THE REAR, BELCHING FROM BEHIND, TOOTING THE TROUSER TRUMPET – WHATEVER YOU CALL IT, WE ALL FART, SOME OF US MORE THAN OTHERS (AND SOME A LOT MORE THAN OTHERS). IF YOU'RE A COMMITTED FARTER – WITH THAT KNOWING SMILE, NEVER SHYING AWAY FROM TAKING FULL RESPONSIBILITY – IT'S TIME YOU GOT THE RECOGNITION YOU DESERVE: A BOOK CELEBRATING YOUR GREATEST SKILL, FULL OF ACTIVITIES AND PUZZLES TO KEEP YOU ENGROSSED, ALONG WITH FASCINATING FART FACTS THAT'LL BLOW YOUR MIND.

THIS PAIR APPEARS ONLY ONCE
ON THE OPPOSITE PAGE

59% NITROGEN

21% HYDROGEN

9% CARBON DIOXIDE

7% METHANE

4% OXYGEN

IF YOU'RE THINKING ABOUT LIGHTING YOUR FARTS (AND WE STRONGLY RECOMMEND THAT YOU DON'T), IT'S THE HYDROGEN AND METHANE THAT ARE FLAMMABLE

IS IT A FART? IS IT A POO? RISK IT!

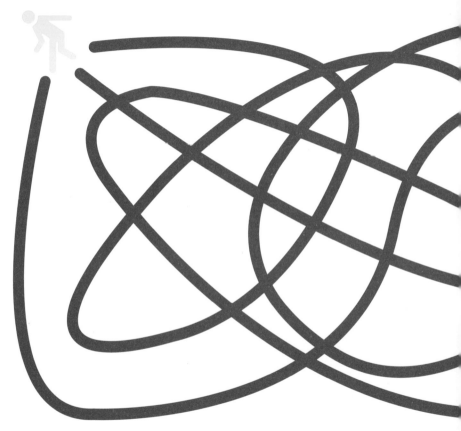

52 THINGS TO DO WHILE YOU POO

FART

FLUFF

BOTTOM BURP

TOOT

GAS

FLATULENCE

RIPPER

PUMP

BREAK WIND

```
Q W K F F C V B B N
B O T T O M B U R P
A S O F G H L K E M
R O F L U F F U A I
T R E P P I R P K O
A S P D F S L H W J
T Q U N P A T U I K
R D M F F G J O N K
A A P C V B N M D L
F L A T U L E N C E
```

IF I COULD LIGHT MY OWN FARTS I COULD FLY TO THE MOON, OR AT LEAST URANUS.

ROBIN WILLIAMS

CREATE SOME
ART IN A FART

TERMITES FART MORE THAN ANY OTHER ORGANISM. GLOBAL EMISSIONS FROM TERMITES MAKE THEM ONE OF THE LARGEST NATURAL SOURCES OF METHANE.

NO FARTING IN THE YOGA STUDIO

THIS PAIR APPEARS ONLY ONCE
ON THE OPPOSITE PAGE

LIGHTING YOUR FARTS IS YOUR PARTY
TRICK BUT YOU'VE DROPPED THE MATCH
INTO THE BOWL OF NIBBLES.
FIND IT BEFORE YOU MISS YOUR CHANCE!

MY PHILOSOPHY OF DATING IS TO JUST FART RIGHT AWAY.

JENNY McCARTHY

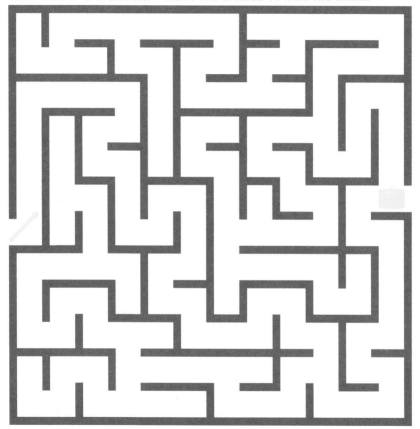

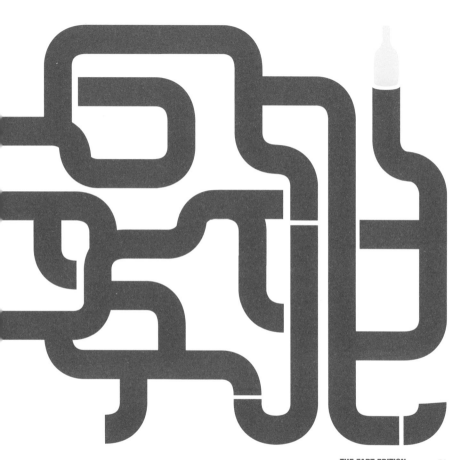

YOU PASS ABOUT HALF A LITRE (17 FL. OZ) OF GAS EACH DAY

BAKED BEANS
CABBAGE
SPROUTS
EGGS
WHOLEGRAIN
PRUNES
ONIONS
FIZZY DRINK
BROCCOLI

A	G	G	H	W	R	B	T	F	U
W	H	O	L	E	G	R	A	I	N
S	U	Y	T	R	P	O	P	Z	S
N	E	G	G	E	R	C	L	Z	P
O	G	E	C	V	U	C	K	Y	R
I	A	W	G	B	N	O	J	D	O
N	B	A	N	G	E	L	G	R	U
O	B	S	D	F	S	I	F	I	T
B	A	K	E	D	B	E	A	N	S
A	C	S	D	F	G	H	J	K	K

IF YOU LET GO OF FART JOKES,
YOU'VE LET GO OF A PIECE
OF HUMANITY.

ANDY SAMBERG

LIKE SUDOKU
BUT WITH FARTS

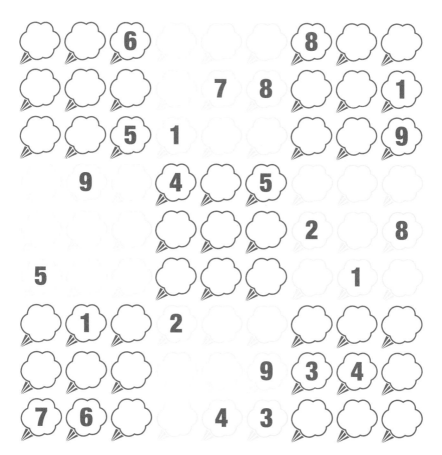

YOU'VE JUST FARTED IN A LIFT.
PICK A FLOOR AND HOPE NO ONE JOINS YOU!

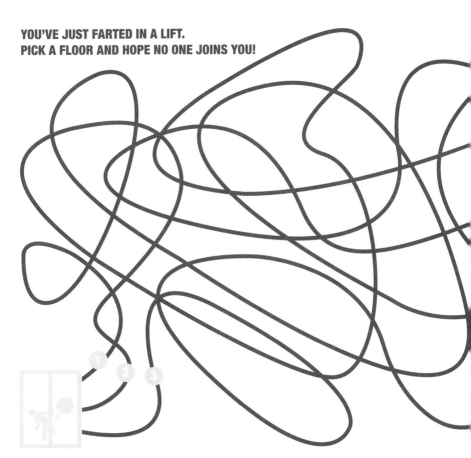

52 THINGS TO DO WHILE YOU POO

A DOG IS NOT INTELLIGENT.
NEVER TRUST AN ANIMAL THAT'S
SURPRISED BY ITS OWN FARTS.

FRANK SKINNER

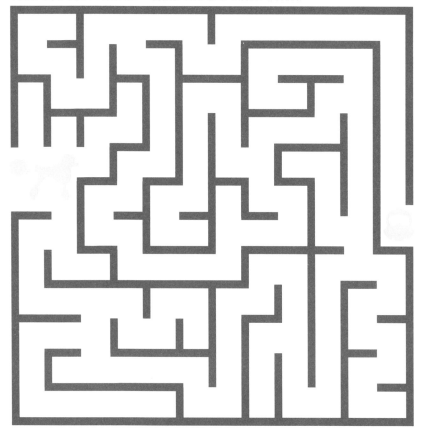

SPOT THE DIFFERENCE – THERE'S ONLY ONE!

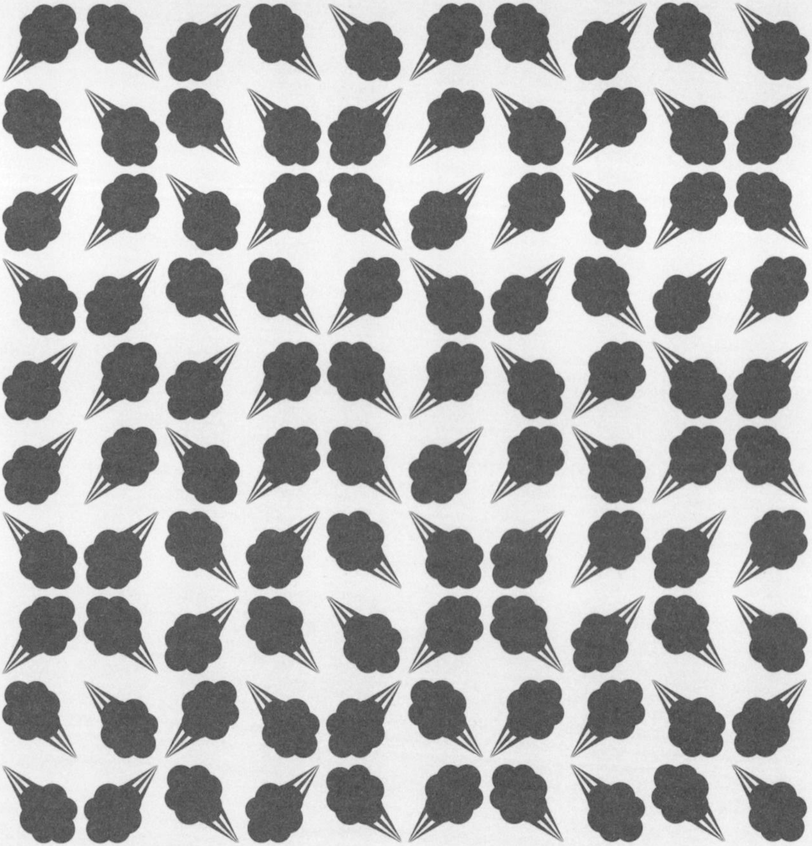

THIS PAIR APPEARS ONLY ONCE ON THE OPPOSITE PAGE

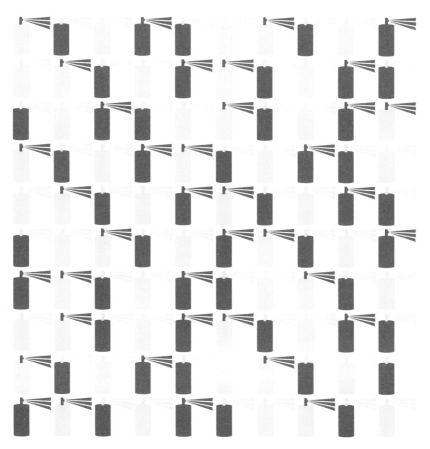

THE AVERAGE PERSON BREAKS WIND ABOUT FOURTEEN TIMES EACH DAY

DESIGN YOUR OWN
FART-FIGHTING FRAGRANCE

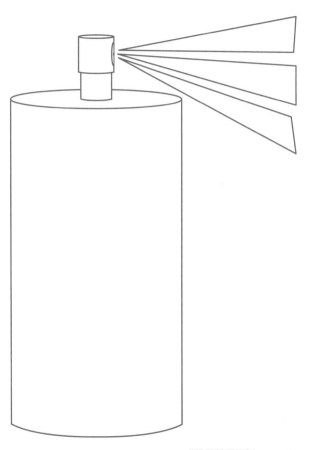

YOU'VE TRIED EVERYTHING!
A CORK IS YOUR LAST RESORT –
FIND ONE IN THE UTENSILS DRAWER

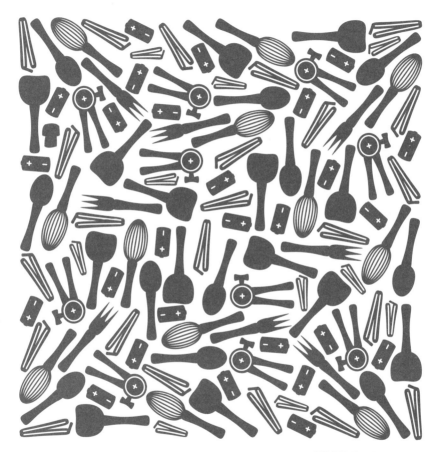

FIND THE FART

```
F R A T F T A R F R T R F A R A F R T R
R F R A T F T A R F R T R F A R A F R T
T R F A R A F R T R F R A T F T A R F R
R T R F R A T F T A R F R T R F T R A F
R F R A T F T A R F R T R F A R A F R T
F R A T F T A R F R T R F A R A F R T R
R T R F R A T F T A R F R T R F A R A F
F R T R F R A T F T A R F R T R F A R A
R A T F T A R F R T R F A R A F R T R F
F R A T F T A R F R T R F A R A F R T R
R F A R A F R T R F R A T F T A R F R T
T R F R A T F T A R F R T R F A R A F R
F R A T F T A R F R T R F A R A F R T R
R A T F T A R F R T R F A R A F R T R F
T R F R A T F T A R F R T R F A R A F R
R T R F R A T F T A R F R T R F A R A F
R A T F A R T F R T R F A R A F R T R F
A T F T A R F R T R F A R A F R T R F R
R F R A T F T A R F R T R F A R A F R T
T R F R A T F T A R F R T R F A R A F R
```

THE FART EDITION

FART QUOTE

CUMBERBATCH – IT SOUNDS LIKE A FART IN A BATH, DOESN'T IT?

BENEDICT CUMBERBATCH

SILENT
LOUD
PROUD
DEADLY
WET
RIPPER
MUFFLED
EXPLOSIVE

52 THINGS TO DO WHILE YOU POO

```
P E M N B V F F U O
F R S I L E N T K P
C N O C O E E R N L
L W R U U W Y E B M
P R O U D Y U P V U
F D S A P O I P C F
G Y L D A E D I X F
H W G F D S A R Z L
K E X P L O S I V E
L T Q W E X B V M D
```

THIS PAIR APPEARS ONLY ONCE
ON THE OPPOSITE PAGE

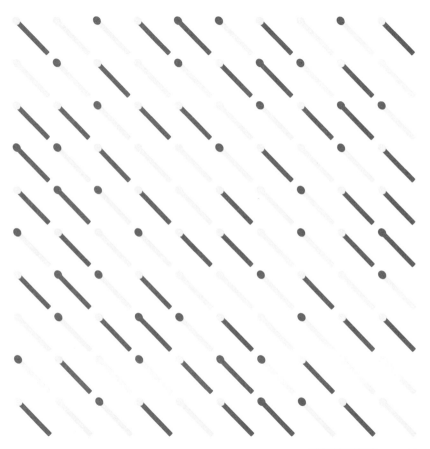

WELCOME TO FART CLUB

WELCOME TO FART CLUB

YOU'VE GOT ONE BREWING – GET TO THE BABY SO YOU CAN SHIFT THE BLAME

FARTS LEAVE THE BODY AT SPEEDS OF UP TO 10 FEET PER SECOND (WHICH IS NEARLY 7 MILES AN HOUR)

LIKE SUDOKU
BUT WITH FARTS

52 THINGS TO DO WHILE YOU POO

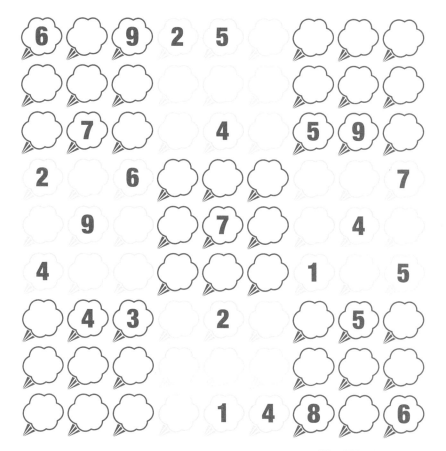

YOU'VE GOT 10 SECONDS

YOU TOOK THE RISK AND YOU WERE WRONG – FIND SOME NEW UNDERPANTS

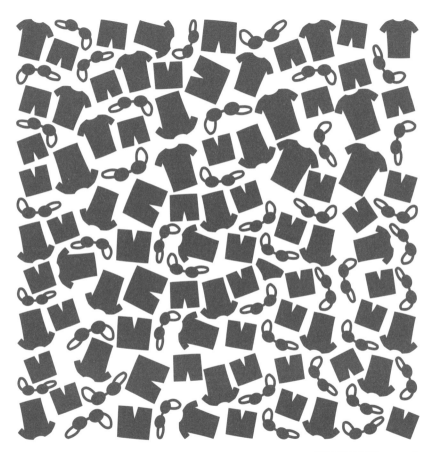

A FART IS JUST
YOUR ARSE
APPLAUDING.

BILLY CONNOLLY

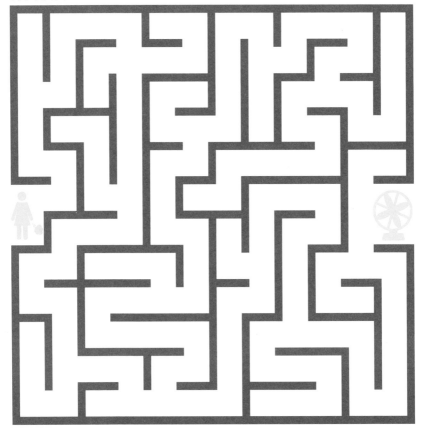

SPOT THE DIFFERENCE – THERE'S ONLY ONE!

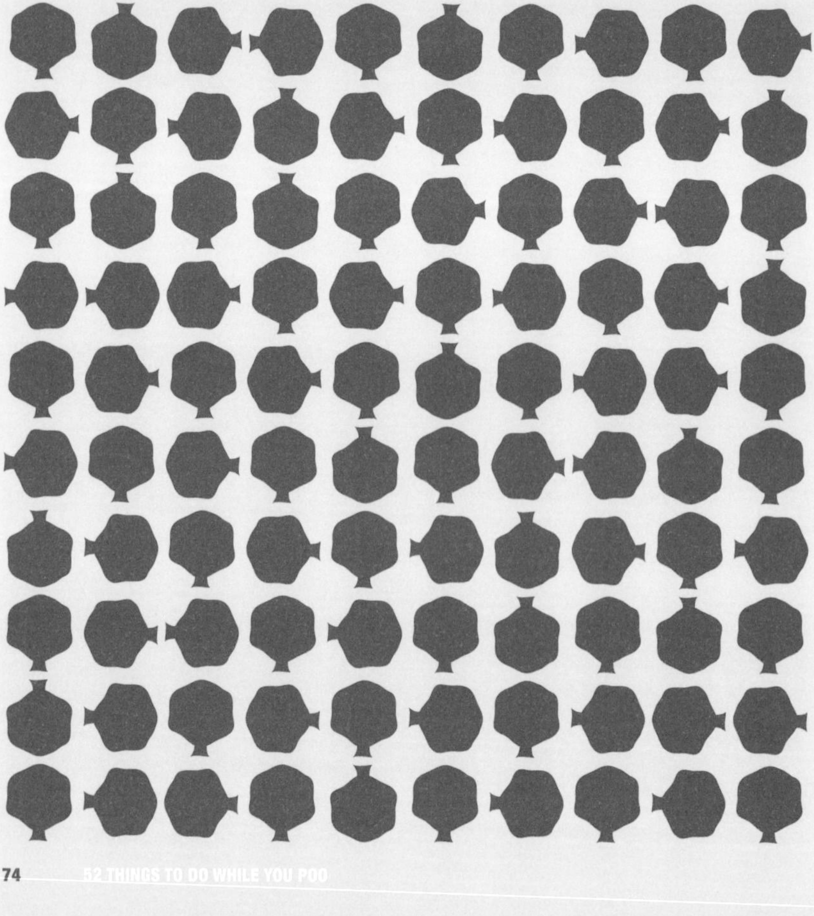

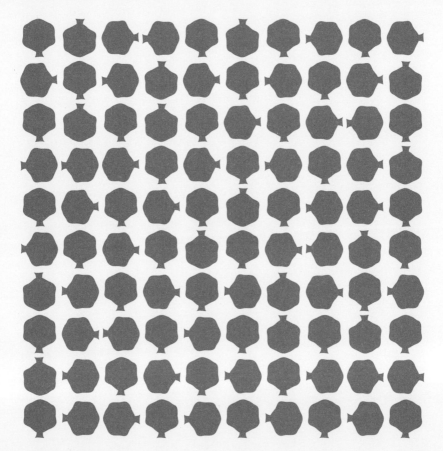

THE YANOMAMI TRIBE IN SOUTH AMERICA FART AS A GREETING

LOCATE THE SMELL

```
S M L E E M S L M S E L L M E S M E M L
E L L M E S M E M L S M L E E M S L M S
E S M E M E M S L M S E L L S M L L E M
E M S L M E S M E M L S M L E L L M E S
L L M E S M S M L E E M S L M S E L L M
M L E E M S M E L L E S M E M L S M L L
E L L S M L E S M E M E M S L M S E L L
S M L E L E E M S L M E S M E M L S M L
L M S E S M L E E M S L M S E L L M E S
E M L S E L L M E S M E M L S M L L E M
S L M S E S M E M E M S L M S E L L S M
M E M L E M S L M E S M E M L S M L E L
M L L E L L M E S M S M L E E M S L M S
L L M E M E L E M S E L L M E S M E M L
S M E M E L L S M L E S M E M E M S L M
M S L M S M L E L E E M S L M E S M E M
L M E S M S M L E E M S L M S E L L M E
E L E M S E L L M E S M E M L S M L L S
L L S M L E S M E M E M S L M S E L L M
M L E E L E M S L M E S M E M L S M L M
```

52 THINGS TO DO WHILE YOU POO

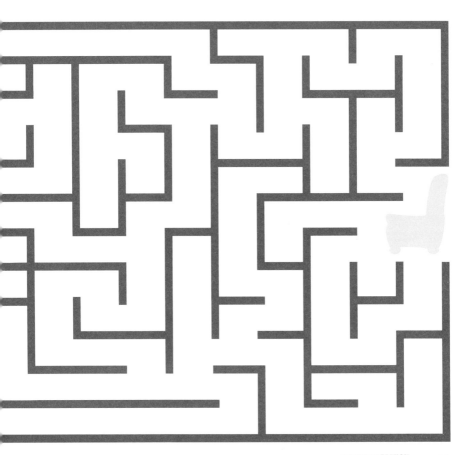

A RELATIONSHIP IS LIKE A FART.
IF YOU PUSH TOO HARD,
THINGS COULD GET MESSY.

KEVIN HART

THE FART EDITION

STINK

SMELL

PONG

STENCH

FRAGRANCE

WHIFF

AROMA

BOUQUET

SCENT

REEK

```
C W H I F F A S D F
R O K E E R I O F P
L A R O G L P M R K
L R E W A R O M A N
E T D R E W N N G I
M Y U I O P G B R T
S T N E C S U V A S
S G W Y N T F F N Q
A Q R T S T E N C H
W F F B O U Q U E T
```

THIS PAIR APPEARS ONLY ONCE
ON THE OPPOSITE PAGE

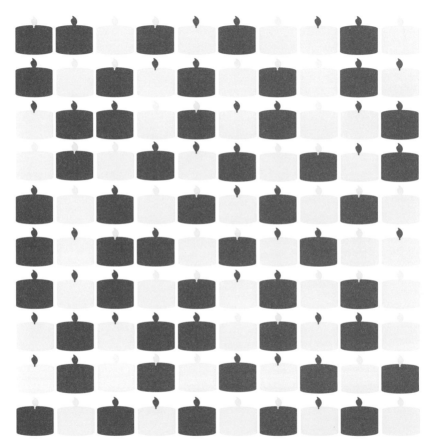

IT IS SAID THAT THE ROMAN EMPEROR CLAUDIUS THOUGHT THAT HOLDING FARTS IN WAS SO UNHEALTHY THAT HE PROPOSED A LAW STATING THAT IT WAS ACCEPTABLE TO BREAK WIND AT BANQUETS

**THE FIRST RULE OF FART CLUB:
YOU DO NOT TALK ABOUT FART CLUB.
BUT SOMEONE HAS – FIND THEM**

SPOT THE DIFFERENCE – THERE'S ONLY ONE!

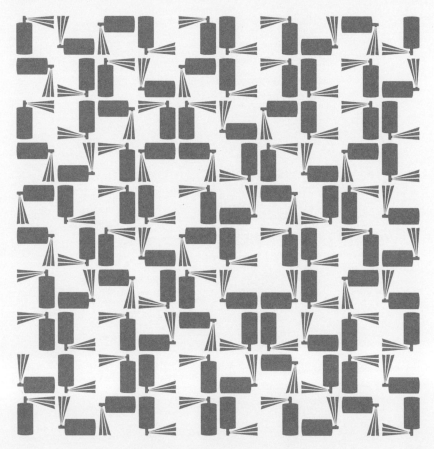

I HAVE iFART ON MY PHONE.
I HAVE REMOTE WHOOPIE CUSHIONS.
FARTS. TO ME, THERE'S
NOTHING FUNNIER.

GEORGE CLOONEY

NO ONE LIKES A FOLLOW-THROUGH – GET SOME PAPER!

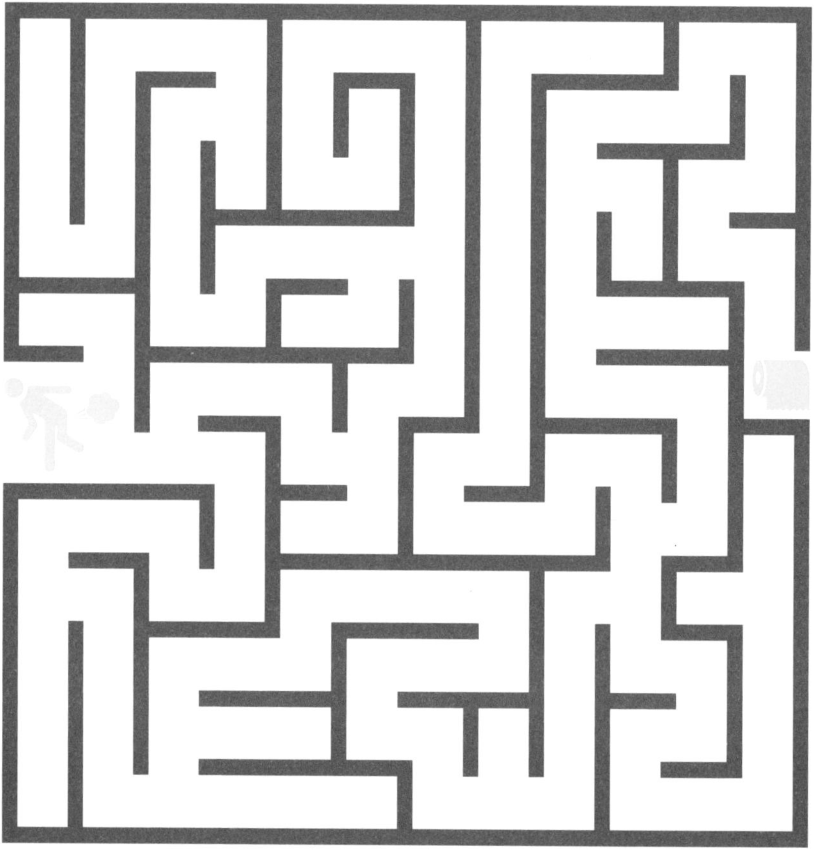

LIKE SUDOKU
BUT WITH FARTS

52 THINGS TO DO WHILE YOU POO

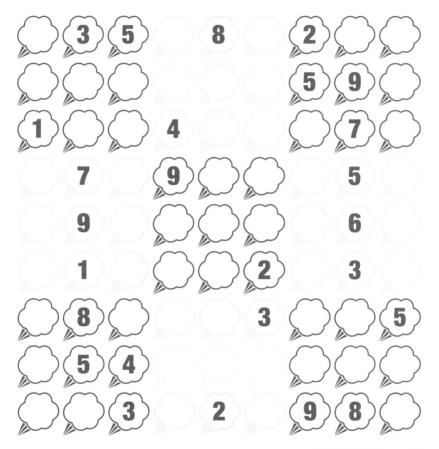

A COUPLE WHO FART TOGETHER STAY TOGETHER – FIND THE HAPPY COUPLE

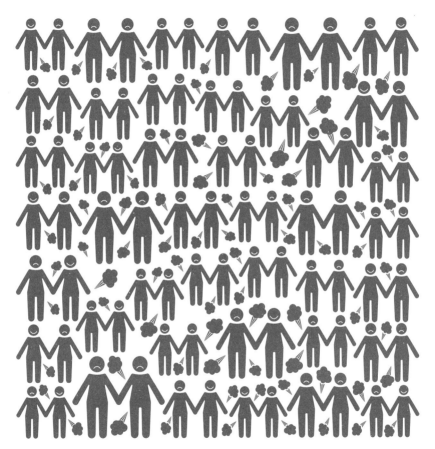

ANSWERS

P6-7

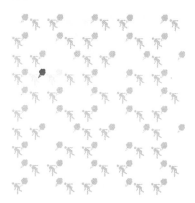

P10-11

52 THINGS TO DO WHILE YOU POO

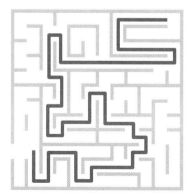

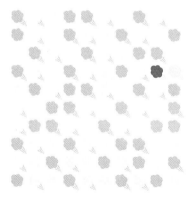

THE FART EDITION

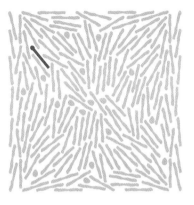

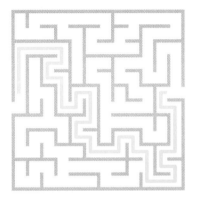

52 THINGS TO DO WHILE YOU POO

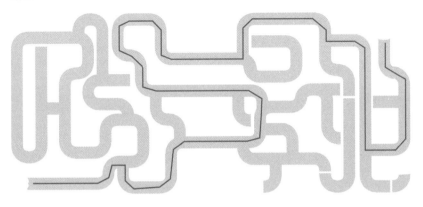

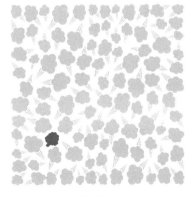

THE FART EDITION 103

52 THINGS TO DO WHILE YOU POO

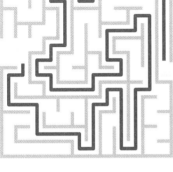

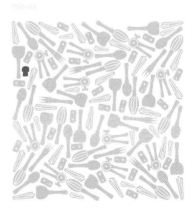

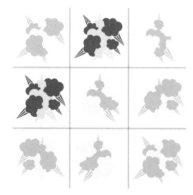

52 THINGS TO DO WHILE YOU POO

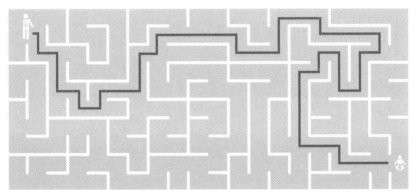

THE FART EDITION 107

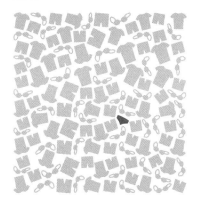

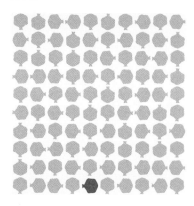

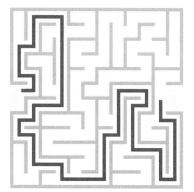

```
S M L E E M S L M S E L L M E S M E M L
E L L M E S M E M L S M L E E M S L M S
E S M E M E M S L M S E L L S M L L E M
E M S L M E S M E M L S M L E L L M E S
L L M E S M S M L E E M S L M S E L L M
M L E E M S M E L L E S M E M L S M L L
E L L S M L E S M E M E M S L M S E L L
S M L E L E E M S L M E S M E M L S M L
L M S E S M L E E M S L M S E L L M E S
E M L S E L L M E S M E M L S M L L E M
S L M S E S M E M E M S L M S E L L S M
M E M L E M S L M E S M E M L S M L E L
M L L E L L M E S M S M L E E M S L M S
L L M E M E L E M S E L L M E S M E M L
S M E M E L L S M L E S M E M E M S L M
M S L L M S M L É L E E M S L M E S M E M
L M E S M S M L E E M S L M S E L L M E
E L E M S E L L M E S M E M L S M L L S
L L S M L E S M E M E M S L M S E L L M
M L E E L E M S L M E S M E M L S M L M
```

52 THINGS TO DO WHILE YOU POO

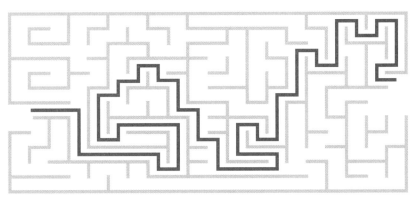

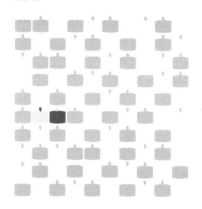

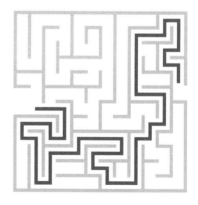

52 THINGS TO DO WHILE YOU POO

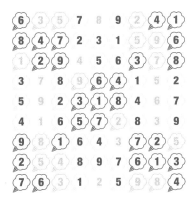

IF YOU'RE INTERESTED IN FINDING OUT MORE
ABOUT OUR BOOKS, FIND US ON FACEBOOK
AT SUMMERSDALE PUBLISHERS AND FOLLOW
US ON TWITTER AT @SUMMERSDALE.

WWW.SUMMERSDALE.COM